S0-AXD-748

This book belongs to:

Name *Patrick Francis Reis*

I was born on *July 16, 1983*.

I was baptized on _____.

I first received Reconciliation on

_____.

I first received Holy Communion on

April 8, 1991.

A Note about this Prayer Book

This prayer book can help you celebrate being
Catholic through
- the Mass,
- the parables of Jesus,
- the sacrament of Reconciliation,
- the seasons and feasts,
- the lives of the saints,
- the Rosary,
- prayers.

You can use this book at home and in church.
Read it with your family and talk about it to
learn more about God, who loves you so
much.

You can follow along when you are at Mass,
when you receive the sacrament of
Reconciliation, when you say the Rosary, and
anytime you want to pray.

This prayer book is your very own. While you
use it, you can talk to God—Father, Son, and
Holy Spirit—and to Mary and the saints.
You can say the short prayers given or you can
make up your own.

A Prayer Book for Young Catholics

Jesus,

TEACH US TO PRAY

BENZIGER PUBLISHING COMPANY
Mission Hills, California

Special Editorial Consultant:
Irene H. Murphy

Illustrations:
Robert Keith Phillips

Nihil Obstat:
Msgr. Joseph Pollard, S.T.D., V.F.
Censor Deputatus

Imprimatur:
†Roger M. Mahony
Archbishop of Los Angeles
May 5, 1989

The nihil obstat and imprimatur are official declarations that a book or
pamphlet is free of doctrinal or moral error. No implication is contained
therein that those who have granted the nihil obstat and imprimatur agree
with the contents, opinions, or statements expressed.

Send all inquiries to:
Benziger Publishing Company
15319 Chatsworth Street, P.O. Box 9509
Mission Hills, California 91345-9509

Printed in the United States of America

ISBN 0-02-653090-2
1 2 3 4 5 6   93 92 91 90 89

Contents

4

The Mass

At Mass, we celebrate.
We sing and pray.
We listen to God's Word.
We receive Jesus.

5

Introductory Rite

The Entrance and Greeting STAND

To begin the Mass, we sing or pray.
The priest and helpers walk to
the altar.
The priest greets us.

Priest: "The Lord be with you."
Us: "And also with you."

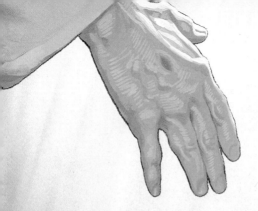

Lord, Have Mercy

We remember how much God loves us.
We feel sorry for doing any wrong.

Priest: "Lord, have mercy."
Us: "Lord, have mercy."

7

The Gloria

STAND

We praise God as the angels did
when Jesus was born.

All: "Glory to God in the highest."

The Liturgy of the Word

The Liturgy of the Word begins.
God will speak to us.
We will learn about following Jesus.

9

The First Reading

We listen to God's Word.
This reading tells us about people
   who lived before Jesus.

Reader: "This is the Word of
         the Lord."

Us: "Thanks be to God."

The Psalm Response

SIT

David the King sang to God.
We join in a song from the Bible.

11

The Second Reading

We listen to another reading.
We listen to the words of one of
    the special friends of Jesus.

Reader: "This is the Word of
    the Lord."

Us: "Thanks be to God."

The Alleluia

STAND

Now, we hear the Good News of Jesus.
We stand and praise God.

Priest: "Alleluia!"
Us: "Alleluia!"

The Gospel

STAND

The deacon or priest reads to us from one of the four Gospels, the Good News of Jesus.

Priest: "This is the gospel of the Lord."

All: "Praise to You, Lord Jesus Christ."

The Homily

SIT

The deacon or priest talks about
   God's Word.
We learn how to be more like Jesus.

15

The Creed

STAND

We believe in the Father, Son, and
Holy Spirit.

All: "We believe in one God."

16

The Prayer of the Faithful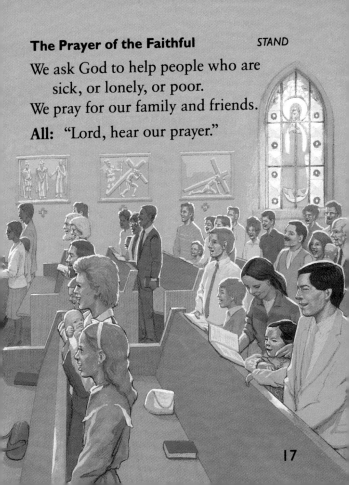

STAND

We ask God to help people who are
   sick, or lonely, or poor.
We pray for our family and friends.

All: "Lord, hear our prayer."

17

The Liturgy of the Eucharist

The Liturgy of the Eucharist begins.
We will remember the death and
   resurrection of Jesus.
We will receive Communion.

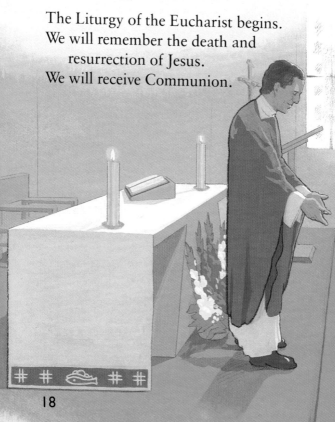

18

The Procession with the Gifts   *SIT*

People bring up gifts.
We offer ourselves to God.

The Preparation of the Gifts *SIT*

We present bread and wine to God.
We ask God to accept our gifts.

All: "Blessed be God forever."

Lift Up Your Hearts

STAND

The priest invites us to join in the thanksgiving prayer.

Priest: "Let us give thanks to the Lord our God."

Us: "It is right to give Him thanks and praise."

21

The Holy, Holy, Holy   STAND

We join our prayer with the song of
the angels and saints.

All: "Holy, holy, holy."

22

The Consecration

KNEEL

The priest says the words of Jesus.
The bread and wine become the Body
   and Blood of Jesus.

Priest: "This is My Body.
        This is the cup of
        My Blood."

23

The Mystery of Faith

KNEEL

We remember that Jesus saved us.

All: "Christ has died.
Christ is risen.
Christ will come again."

24

The Great Amen

KNEEL

We pray for everyone.
We pray to God the Father through
   Jesus and the Holy Spirit.

All: "Amen."

The Lord's Prayer *STAND*

We are God's children.
We say a prayer Jesus taught us.

All: "Our Father."

26

The Sign of Peace

STAND

We get ready to receive Communion.
We show that we love one another.
We share a sign of peace.

Priest: "Peace be with you."
Us: "And also with you."

The Breaking of the Bread   *STAND*

The priest breaks the Host. We
remember the sacrifice
of Jesus.

Priest: "Lamb of God,
You take away the sins of
the world, grant us peace."

28

The Prayer before Communion STAND

We get ready to receive Jesus.

All: "Lord, I am not worthy to receive You, but only say the word and I shall be healed."

29

Communion

We receive Communion.

Priest: "The Body of Christ."

Us: "Amen."

The Silent Prayer
after Communion   *SIT*

After Communion, we thank Jesus for
   all His love.
We ask for help to love everyone.

The Final Blessing STAND

The priest blesses us.
We are sent to help everyone.

Priest: "Go in peace to love and
serve the Lord."

Us: "Thanks be to God."

The Parables

Jesus told teaching stories called parables.
They teach us how to live as God asks us to.
They help us to love God and one another.

33

"The Salt of the Earth" and "The Lamp on a Stand"

(Matthew 5:13–16)

Salt makes things taste better.
Just one lamp can light up a room.

Lord Jesus, I can be as helpful as
salt. Help me let Your goodness
shine as I help others.

34

"The Seed and the Yeast"
(Matthew 13:31–33)

Showing God's love is like a tiny
    seed that grows into a big plant.
It is like the little pinch of
    yeast that makes bread dough rise.

Holy Spirit, help me to do little
kindnesses. They can make a big
difference to people.

35

"The Workers in the Vineyard"
(Matthew 20:1–16)

At dawn, a man hired some workers
   to pick grapes.
During the day, the man hired more
   and more people.
At sunset, all got a full day's pay.
Some workers said, "But we worked
   all day! They worked just an hour!"
The man said, "It's my money. I can
   be generous with it."

Thank You, God, for what You give me.

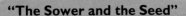

"The Sower and the Seed"

(Mark 4:1–9)

A farmer scattered some seeds.
Some of the seeds fell on the path,
    on rocks, or in thorns.
These seeds did not grow.
Other seeds fell on good ground and
    grew wonderfully.
These seeds grew into big plants
    that gave many, many seeds.

Lord Jesus, may Your love grow in
me so that I do many good things.

37

"The Good Samaritan"
(Luke 10:29–37)

A man was going home.
But robbers beat him and left him
    hurt by the road.
An important man passed by, but he
    didn't help.
Another person passed by, too.
Then came a man from another
    country.
He cared for the hurt man.

Holy Spirit, help me to
be kind to people who do not
have friends.

"The Friend Who Kept Trying"
(Luke 11:5–10)

One night, a friend knocked on a
   man's door when he was in bed.
He did not want to get up.
The friend called out, "I need some
   bread for a visitor."
The man still did not get up.
But, the friend kept knocking.
At last, the man got up and gave
   the friend as much as was
   needed.

Dear God, help
me to keep on
asking You when
I need something.

"The Lost Sheep and the Lost Coin"

(Luke 15:1–10)

When a sheep was lost, the shepherd
 kept looking until he found it.
Then, he was so happy, he carried
 it home.
A woman lost some money.
She searched until it was found.
Both people were happy to find what
 was lost.

Lord Jesus, sometimes I forget You
and I am not loving. I am sorry. I
want to be happy with You forever.

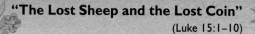

"The Prodigal Son"
(Luke 15:11–32)

A young man said to his father,
   "Give me my half of your money."
The young man left his father and
   wasted the money doing bad things.
Then, he was so hungry, he got a
   job feeding pigs.
At last, he said, "I was wrong.
   I'll tell my father I'm sorry."
The father was looking for his son.
When he saw his son, he ran and
   welcomed the boy with great love.

Holy Spirit, help me to say "I'm
sorry." Help me to
forgive others.

41

"The Pharisee and the Tax Collector"

(Luke 18:9–14)

Two men went to a holy place.
The first man prayed, "I'm so good!"
The second one prayed, "Dear God, I
    am sorry for my sins."
Which was the better prayer?

Lord Jesus, help me to be a good
friend to You.

The Sacrament of Reconciliation

 Jesus said to love God with all your heart, soul, strength, and mind.
This is the greatest commandment. The second is to love each person as much as you love yourself.

God asks us to be close friends with one another and with God. Sometimes we do not do as God wants. We need to say that we are sorry and try to be more like Jesus. The sacrament of Reconciliation welcomes us back to a close friendship with people and God.

Examination of Conscience

I remember my good and bad actions.

Dear Holy Spirit,
Help me answer these questions:
- Do I talk to God every day?
- Do I help others as Jesus did?
- Do I do things that will help me grow as God wants?
- Do I take care of what I have?
- Do I obey good rules?
- Am I always honest in games, on schoolwork, and at home?
- Do I say "I am sorry" and "I forgive you"?

Reading the Word of God

After I examine my conscience, I
    greet the priest.
I make the Sign of the Cross.
The priest may read to me from
    God's Word.
The Word of God helps me to love
    and trust God.

Confession and Penance

I tell the priest how long it has
    been since my last confession.
Then, I tell the priest my sins.
I say why I have not shown love.
The priest listens carefully.
He talks to me to help me be more
    like Jesus.
Then, the priest tells me something
    I can do to try to be better.
This is called a "penance."
I promise to do it.

Act of Contrition

I say an Act of Contrition:

Lord Jesus, Son of God, have mercy on me, a sinner.

or

Dear God, I am sorry for all my sins. I am sorry for doing wrong things and failing to do good things. I will try to do better. Help me to show Your love. Amen.

or

O my God, I am heartily sorry for having offended Thee and I detest all my sins because of Thy just punishment, but most of all because they offend Thee, my God, who are all good, and deserving of all my love. I firmly resolve with the help of Thy grace, to sin no more, and to avoid the near occasions of sin. Amen.

47

Absolution

With his hand, the priest makes a sign
    of forgiveness.
He says, "I absolve you from all
    your sins in the name of the
Father, and of the Son, and of the
    Holy Spirit."
I say, "Amen."
God completely frees me from all
    sin and gives me grace.

Closing Prayer

The priest says, "Give thanks to
   the Lord, for He is good."
I say, "His mercy endures forever."
The priest tells me to go in peace.
I say, "Amen."

Doing the Penance

I do the penance the priest gave me.
With God's help, I try to do better.

Seasons and Feasts

Each year, there are special times to celebrate. In church and at home, we celebrate seasons and feasts.

"Seasons" are holy times that last for several weeks.

"Feasts" are special holy days.

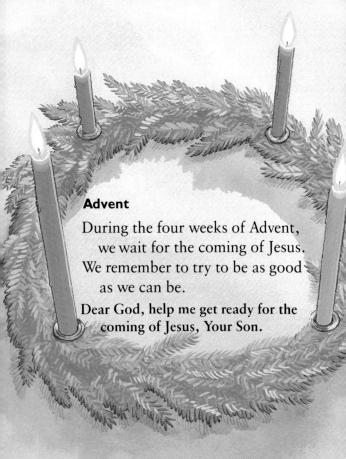

Advent

During the four weeks of Advent,
    we wait for the coming of Jesus.
We remember to try to be as good
    as we can be.

Dear God, help me get ready for the
    coming of Jesus, Your Son.

Christmas

On Christmas Day, we celebrate the
birth of Jesus.
Glory to God and peace to everyone!

Holy Spirit, help us live in peace.

During Lent, we think about how we
    can be better friends of Jesus.
We make good changes in our lives.
We get ready to celebrate Easter.

Dear Jesus, I am sorry for the
times I have not shown love. Help
me to keep trying to be like You.

Holy Thursday

On Holy Thursday, Jesus shared His
Last Supper with His friends.
At the Last Supper, Jesus changed
bread and wine into His Body
and Blood.

Dear Jesus, thank You for giving us
the Eucharist. Help me to receive
Communion often.

Good Friday

On Good Friday, Jesus died on the cross out of love for us.

I love You, Jesus. Help me always to remember how much You love me.

Easter

Three days after His death, Jesus
rose from the dead.

On Easter Sunday, we are very happy
because Jesus shares His new life
with us.

Dear God, You give us new life! Alleluia!

57

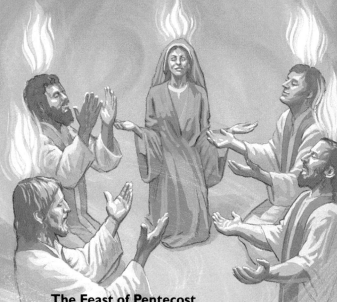

The Feast of Pentecost

Fifty days after Easter

On Pentecost, we celebrate the day
the Holy Spirit came to the friends
of Jesus.

Come, Holy Spirit, fill me with
love. Help me to be like Jesus.

The Feast of the Assumption

At the end of her life, Mary was
    taken, body and soul, into heaven.

Dear Mary, my Mother, help me
always to trust God like you did.

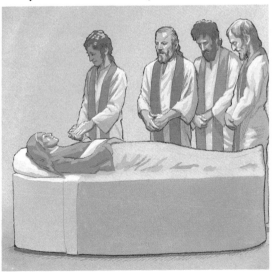

The Feast of All Saints

We do not know all the names of
   people who have loved as Jesus did.
People from all ways of life have
   become saints.
God's Family celebrates every saint.

**All the saints, pray for me! Help
me, too, be a good friend of God.**

The Feast of the
Immaculate Conception

December 8

"Immaculate" means free from sin.
"The Immaculate Conception" is a
special name for Mary,
the Mother of God.
She was always free from sin.
She is the patron saint of the
United States.
"Patron" means "a special helper."

Immaculate Mary, pray for the
people in the United States.

The Feast of Our Lady of Guadalupe

December 12

Mary appeared to an Aztec Indian
    named Juan.
She told him she would be the
    Mother of his people.
Suddenly, a picture of Mary was
    on his cloak.
She is the patron saint
    of the Americas and
    the Philippines.

**Our Lady of Guadalupe,
help me to care for the poor.**

The Saints

Saints are people who tried hard to help everyone as Jesus did. We can talk to them and ask for help. Some saints are special helpers called "patron" saints. Your patron saint is the saint you were named for.

Saint Elizabeth Ann Seton

January 4

Saint Elizabeth Ann Seton was born
    in New York City.
She was a wife and mother.
Later, she became a Sister.
She started the first Catholic school in
    the United States.

Saint Elizabeth Ann Seton, help me
to do my best in school.

Saint Patrick

Saint Patrick was an Irish bishop.
He told the Good News of Jesus.
Saint Patrick taught about the
    Blessed Trinity, the three Persons
    in one God.

**Saint Patrick, help me to love
God—the Father, the Son, and the
Holy Spirit.**

65

Saint Joseph

Saint Joseph was Mary's husband.
He worked hard as a carpenter.
He took good care of Jesus.

**Saint Joseph, be with me when I am
working. Help me to do a good job.**

Saint Mark

Saint Mark wrote one of the four
    Gospels that tell the Good News.
He was a good friend of Saint Peter.

Saint Mark, help me to love the
Gospel. Help me to understand the
teachings of Jesus.

Saint Catherine of Siena

April 29

Saint Catherine of Siena helped
    people not to fight.
She helped the poor and the sick.
She wrote about God.

Saint Catherine, help me to work
for peace by saying "I'm sorry" and
"I forgive you."

68

Saint Isidore and Saint Maria

Saint Isidore and his wife Saint
    Maria lived in Spain.
They worked on a farm.
Isidore and Maria were poor.
But they shared whatever they had
    with other people.

Saint Isidore and Saint Maria, help
all people have enough to eat. Help
me to share what I have.

Saint Anthony of Padua

June 13

Saint Anthony was a priest and a
    great preacher.
He was a follower of Saint Francis.
Once, the child Jesus appeared to
    Saint Anthony.
Many people pray to Saint Anthony
    for help finding things.

**Saint Anthony, help me to find
Jesus in everyone.**

The Birth of Saint John the Baptist

June 24

When Saint John grew up,
   he baptized people.
He helped them to get ready for the
   Good News of Jesus.
Saint John, help me to tell the
truth always.

71

Saint Peter and Saint Paul

June 29

Jesus asked Saint Peter to be the
    leader of the Apostles.
Saint Peter became the first pope.
Saint Paul taught many people to
    believe in Jesus.
Saint Peter and Saint Paul both
    gave their lives for Jesus.

Saint Peter and Saint Paul, help me
to do what Jesus asks, even when it
is hard.

Saint Mary Magdalene

July 22

Saint Mary Magdalene was a helper
of Jesus and one of His friends.
When Jesus rose from the dead, He
appeared to Saint Mary first.

Saint Mary Magdalene, when I am
worried, help me turn to Jesus.

73

Saint Joachim and Saint Anne

July 26

Saint Joachim and Saint Anne were
Mary's father and mother.
They were the grandparents of Jesus.
Saint Joachim and Saint Anne taught
Mary about God.

**Saint Joachim and Saint Anne, pray for
my family and me.**

Saint Maximilian Kolbe

August 14

Saint Maximilian was a priest who
loved Mary very much.
When Saint Maximilian was put into
prison, he helped the people there.
He even gave his life to save
another prisoner.

Saint Maximilian, when I am afraid,
help me to do what is right.

75

Saint Augustine

When Saint Augustine was young, he
 did many things wrong.
But his mother, Saint Monica,
 prayed for him.
He realized he needed to change.
He asked God to forgive him.
He became a great bishop.
He taught and wrote about God.

Saint Augustine and Saint Monica,
help all families when they are
having hard times. Help me to say
"I'm sorry" when I do wrong.

Saint Matthew

Saint Matthew was an Apostle.
The twelve Apostles were the first
  followers of Jesus.
Saint Matthew wrote a Gospel
  telling the Good News about Jesus.

Saint Matthew, help me to follow the
teachings of Jesus.

Saint Vincent de Paul

September 27

Saint Vincent de Paul was a very
   kind priest.
He lived in France.
He cared for the poor and helped
   young men become priests.

**Saint Vincent, help me be kind to
all people.**

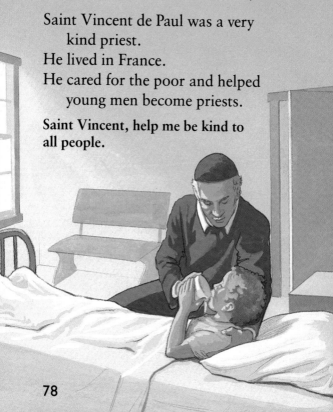

Saint Michael, Saint Gabriel, and Saint Raphael

September 29

Saint Michael, Saint Gabriel, and
  Saint Raphael are three of the
  angels, God's special helpers.
The angels always obey God.
Your guardian angel helps you.
Saint Michael fights against wrong.
Saint Gabriel is God's messenger.
Saint Raphael helps travelers.

Saint Michael, Saint Gabriel, and Saint Raphael, and my guardian angel, help me to obey God.

79

Saint Thérèse of the Child Jesus

October 1

Saint Thérèse was a nun.
She worked and prayed and offered
   everything she did to God.
She taught us to do little things
   well because we love God.
Saint Thérèse, help me to do even
little things with love.

Saint Francis of Assisi

October 4

Saint Francis gave up all his
things to become poor like Jesus.
Saint Francis knew that everything
in the world is a gift from God.

Saint Francis, help me to take good
care of God's world.

81

Saint Luke

Saint Luke was a doctor and a
   helper of Saint Paul.
Saint Luke wrote the third Gospel.
Luke's Gospel tells how much God
   loves the poor.

Saint Luke, help me to be fair.
Help me to work for peace.

Saint Martin de Porres

November 3

Saint Martin was a Brother who
    lived in South America.
He prayed for the poor and sick.
He helped them.
Saint Martin also cared for animals.

**Saint Martin, help me care for my
pets and other animals.**

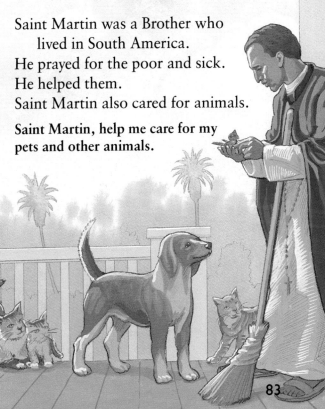

Saint Frances Xavier Cabrini

November 13

Saint Frances Cabrini was a Sister
from Italy.
She came to the United States to
help the poor and the sick.
She helped start many orphanages
and schools.

Saint Frances Cabrini, help me to
be as generous with my time as
you were.

Saint Elizabeth of Hungary

November 17

Saint Elizabeth was happily married
to a German king.
After her husband died, she gave up
her riches.
Saint Elizabeth always helped
the poor.

Saint Elizabeth, help me to accept
not having everything I want. Help
me to give to others.

Saint Francis Xavier

December 3

Saint Francis Xavier was
    a missionary.
A missionary goes to other lands to
    teach people about Jesus.
Saint Francis Xavier is the patron
    of the missions.

**Saint Francis Xavier, help me to
tell people about Jesus.**

Saint Nicholas

December 6

Saint Nicholas was a bishop.
He always helped people,
    especially children.
He is the patron of children.

**Saint Nicholas, help me to share,
like you did.**

87

Saint John

December 27

Saint John was the youngest Apostle.
He was a close friend of Jesus.
The fourth Gospel is by Saint John.
His Gospel teaches us to love Jesus.

**Saint John, help me to listen to
the Gospel carefully.**

The Rosary

The Rosary helps us think about fifteen "mysteries," wonders that God has done through Jesus and Mary.

To say the Rosary:

1. Hold the cross. Say the Apostles' Creed. Go on to the first bead. Say the Lord's Prayer. On the next three beads, say three Hail Marys. Then, say one Glory to the Father.

2. Say the name of the mystery. Say one Lord's Prayer. On the ten little beads, say ten Hail Marys. On the bead by itself, say one Glory to the Father. This is saying a "decade."

3. Then, repeat Step 2 until you say all five mysteries.

The Joyful Mysteries

For five decades of the Rosary, we remember the Joyful Mysteries of Jesus and Mary.

1. The angel Gabriel announces to Mary she will be God's Mother.
2. Mary visits her cousin Elizabeth.
3. Jesus is born in a stable.
4. Mary and Joseph present Jesus to God in the Temple.
5. Mary and Joseph find Jesus with the teachers in the Temple.

The Sorrowful Mysteries

For five decades of the Rosary, we
    remember the Sorrowful Mysteries
    of Jesus and Mary.

1. Jesus is in agony in the garden.
2. Jesus is scourged.
3. Jesus is crowned with thorns.
4. Jesus carries His cross.
5. Jesus dies on the cross.

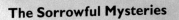

The Glorious Mysteries

For five decades of the Rosary, we
remember the Glorious Mysteries of
Jesus and Mary.

1. Jesus rises from the dead.
2. Jesus ascends to His Father.
3. The Holy Spirit descends on the friends of Jesus.
4. Mary is assumed into heaven.
5. Mary is crowned Queen of heaven and earth.

Prayers

Special times to pray are:
- In the morning and at bedtime
- Before and after meals.
- Anytime you want to say to God: "Help me," "I love You," "Thank You," or "I'm sorry"

Special people to pray for are:
- Your family and friends
- Sick, poor, or homeless people
- The pope and all people who are trying to do what God asks

Prayer for My Family
Lord Jesus, live within my family and help us show Your love. Amen.

Prayer at Bedtime
God, I am sorry for all my sins. Be with me tonight and always. Amen.

The Apostles' Creed

I believe in God, the Father almighty, Creator of heaven and earth. I believe in Jesus Christ, His only Son, our Lord. He was conceived by the power of the Holy Spirit, and born of the Virgin Mary; He suffered under Pontius Pilate, was crucified, died, and was buried. He descended to the dead. On the third day, He rose again. He ascended into heaven, and is seated at the right hand of the Father. He will come again to judge the living and the dead. I believe in the Holy Spirit, the holy catholic Church, the communion of saints, the forgiveness of sins, the resurrection of the body, and life everlasting. Amen.

The Lord's Prayer

Our Father, who art in heaven, hallowed be Thy name. Thy kingdom come; Thy will be done on earth as it is in heaven. Give us this day our daily bread, and forgive us our trespasses as we forgive those who trespass against us. And lead us not into temptation but deliver us from evil. Amen.

The Hail Mary

Hail Mary, full of grace, the Lord is with thee. Blessed art thou among women, and blessed is the Fruit of thy womb, Jesus. Holy Mary, Mother of God, pray for us sinners, now, and at the hour of our death. Amen.

Glory to the Father
Glory to the Father, and to the Son, and to the Holy Spirit. As it was in the beginning, is now, and will be forever. Amen.

An Act of Contrition
Lord Jesus, Son of God, have mercy on me, a sinner.

Grace before Meals
Bless us, O Lord, and these Your gifts, which we are about to receive from Your bounty, through Christ our Lord. Amen.

Grace after Meals
We thank You, O God, for these gifts and for all the gifts we have received from Your goodness, through Christ our Lord. Amen.

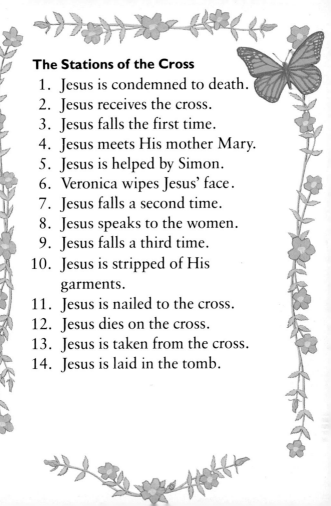

The Stations of the Cross

1. Jesus is condemned to death.
2. Jesus receives the cross.
3. Jesus falls the first time.
4. Jesus meets His mother Mary.
5. Jesus is helped by Simon.
6. Veronica wipes Jesus' face.
7. Jesus falls a second time.
8. Jesus speaks to the women.
9. Jesus falls a third time.
10. Jesus is stripped of His garments.
11. Jesus is nailed to the cross.
12. Jesus dies on the cross.
13. Jesus is taken from the cross.
14. Jesus is laid in the tomb.